The New York Times

THE BOARD OF DIRECTORS
25 KEYS TO CORPORATE GOVERNANCE

MARIANNE JENNINGS, J.D.
Arizona State University

Lebhar-Friedman Books
NEW YORK • CHICAGO • LOS ANGELES • LONDON • PARIS • TOKYO

For *The New York Times*
Mike Levitas, Editorial Director, Book Development
Tom Redburn, General Series Editor
Brent Bowers, Series Editor
James Schembari, Series Editor

Lebhar-Friedman Books
425 Park Avenue
New York, NY 10022

Published by Lebhar-Friedman Books
Lebhar-Friedman Books is a company of Lebhar-Friedman Inc.

Printed in the United States of America

Library of Congress Cataloging-in-Publication Data
Jennings, Marianne.
    The board of directors : 25 keys to corporate governance /
Marianne Jennings.
    p.   cm.—(The New York Times pocket MBA series ; vol. 12)
    Includes index.
    ISBN 0-86730-781-1 (paperback)
    1. Boards of directors.   2. Corporate governance.   I. Title.
II. Series.
    HD2745 .J44   1999
    658.4'22—dc21   99-27692
                                                              CIP

DESIGN & PRODUCTION BY MILLER WILLIAMS DESIGN ASSOCIATES

Visit our Web site at lfbooks.com

INTRODUCTION

LEBHAR-FRIEDMAN BOOKS is proud to present *The New York Times* Pocket MBA Series, 12 invaluable reference volumes that are easily accessible to all businesspersons, from first level managers to the executive suite. The books are written by Ph.D.s who teach in the MBA programs in some of the finest schools in the country. A team of business editors from *The New York Times*— Mike Levitas, Tom Redburn, Brent Bowers, and James Schembari—provided their own expertise to edit a reference series that is beyond compare.

The New York Times Pocket MBA Series offers quick-reference key points learned in top MBA programs. The 25-key structure of each volume presents an unparalleled synopsis of crucial principles of specific areas of business expertise. The unique approach to this series packages academic books for consumers in an easy-to-use trade format that is ideal for the individual businessperson as well as an excellent training reference manual. Be sure to get all 12 titles in the series to complete your own MBA education.

Joseph Mills
Senior Managing Editor
Lebhar-Friedman Books

The New York Times Pocket MBA
Series includes these 12 volumes:

Analyzing Financial Statements

Business Planning

Business Financing

Growing & Managing a Business

Organizing a Company

Forecasting Budgets

Tracking & Controlling Costs

Sales & Marketing

Managing Investment

Going Global

Leadership & Vision

The Board of Directors

25 KEYS TO CORPORATE GOVERNANCE

CONTENTS

KEY 1 The corporation: a beast with unlimited potential and limited liability . . . . page 9

KEY 2 What is a board of directors and why do you need one? . . . . page 12

KEY 3 The board does a lot more than just collect a fee . . . . page 16

KEY 4 Who picks the board members and why do they pick them? . . . . page 19

KEY 5 Electing board members is still the shareholder's job . . . page 26

KEY 6 Tenure for directors is not a good idea . . . . page 30

KEY 7 Compensation in theory and practice: do directors deserve what they earn? . . . . page 33

KEY 8 Pink slips for directors . . . . . . page 36

KEY 9 Directors' fiduciary duty:
it's not their money .... page 38

KEY 10 Mistakes or errors
of judgment? .... page 41

KEY 11 *Carpe diem*, but not the
opportunity .... page 44

KEY 12 Conflicts, contracts and
independent directors .... page 46

KEY 13 On being sued: directors'
liability and insurance ...... page 49

KEY 14 On being sued personally:
directors without
insurance .... page 52

KEY 15 Federal laws and criminal
sanctions: the SEC and other
things that can go bump in
the boardroom .... page 55

KEY 16 Inside information:
the law on juicy tidbits ...... page 58

KEY 17 Who's in charge here? ...... page 61

KEY 18 Board commitees: extra fees
or real purpose? .... page 65

KEY 19 On the board's responsibility
for preventing the books
from being cooked .... page 68

KEY 20 Board meetings: art, science
and requirements .... page 72

KEY 21 Shareholders versus
stakeholders .... page 74

KEY 22 The irate shareholder:
annual ruckus .... page 78

KEY 23 Board reform:
rebels at the gate .... page 81

KEY 24 Good questions for
good board members .... page 85

KEY 25 The best and worst in
corporate boards .... page 88

The corporation: a beast with unlimited potential and limited liability

When first introduced to the novel concept of corporations as a means for financing and operating a business, Adam Smith concluded that they would prove to be dysfunctional beasts. Smith, the 18th century expounder of the virtues of capitalism, thought such a business venture, with so many owners, could not possibly succeed.

Adam Smith may have been right about capitalism, but the great economist was wrong about corporations. They are the heart of American business.

Corporations first existed in the Middle Ages for the operation of towns, universities and ecclesiastical orders—for the good of the whole, those with common interests joined together to operate their enterprises. In municipal, educational and religious corporations, individual members pooled resources and reaped the rewards. The publicly-supported monks tilled the garden, the parishioners ate. The city collected taxes to build the roads and the residents benefited from fewer wheel replacements. The universities operated the libraries and the citizens had access to books. With the development of commerce, the corporate operation migrated to the business world. Those with ideas produced and sold goods using investor funds and those investors (shareholders) split the profits.

Suddenly with this new corporate beast which allowed easy investment by multiple owners, economic growth knew no bounds.

Moreover, the birth of this new commercial creature brought with it the bonus of limited liability. If a corporation is created properly and operated well, the only liability its owners, the shareholders, face is the loss of their investment in the firm. In a well-run corporation, none of the personal assets of any shareholder is subject to the claims of the corporation's creditors. Without such protection, there would be much less investment. With it, this combination of many investors furnishing capital collectively without the risk of losing their own personal shirts has been sufficient motivation to finance everything from a voyage to a new world to the Model-T.

First seen in the United States with the Pilgrims and their Mayflower Company, corporations have continued their dominance of American business. They have created jobs, wealth, culture and a financial market that is now a depository for the funds of most working and retired adults. Americans in particular find corporations to be quite an efficient way to run a business and certainly a welcome entrée into the world of capital gains and dividends.

A corporation is a statutory creature. It requires

the proper public filing of a document, called articles of incorporation, that identifies its creators (called incorporators) and provides information on its structure and purpose. Articles of incorporation list the name of the corporation, its classes and types of shares and includes the name of a contact person for communication with the company. Once the articles of incorporation are filed properly and any additional steps, such as public notice of incorporation are complete, the newly formed entity is recognized by the state as a corporation.

Those who have invested in the corporation and own an interest—the shareholders—enjoy the limited liability afforded this creature of the state dating back to 15th century England.

Shareholders' limited liability, however, is in jeopardy if they fail to treat the property and funds of the corporation as separate. The operation of a corporation requires formalities in everything from approval of transactions to filing annual reports. It would be impossible for a corporation if 50, let alone 10,000, shareholders were left to manage operations and fulfill the formality requirements. The duty of compliance and management of the corporation is delegated by the shareholders to the board of directors, who in turn can delegate responsibility to officers and employees.

The following keys examine the role of the shareholders, directors and officers in running a successful corporation. Corporations are magnificent beasts, which, if governed properly, provide maximum return on investment with little personal risk.

What is a board of directors and why do you need one?

Adam Smith was not only wrong about corporations, he was wrong about the ability of corporate boards to watch with anxious vigilance. His fear may have sprung from the idea that those minding the store might be tempted to slack off, or, even worse, dip into the till while on guard duty. Adam Smith underestimated the creativity and motivation of armies of business and legal minds who, over the years, have developed a variety of ways to curb dipping and slacking among managers.

When a corporation is created by its shareholder owners, it becomes what the law falteringly refers to as a "fictitious person." By law, fictitious persons have nearly all the same rights that a natural, even shallow, person might have. Corporations can own property and enter into contracts, but they must pay taxes, too. Corporations cannot take the Fifth Amendment as a defense against releasing corporate documents, but they are entitled to all other rights and responsibilities under the law.

The truly tricky part of being a fictitious person with many rights is the inability to speak up. When a real person is being robbed, he tends to speak, rather loudly, about the theft of his property. A fictitious person is at the mercy of natural persons when it comes to being robbed. And real people gathered around the funds of a corporation might be tempted to divert them or use its resources to their own benefit at the expense of the shareholders. People in corporations who have not been adequately supervised can get away with murder. They have done everything from the illegal—Michael Monus, for example, embezzled funds by keeping two sets of books at Phar-Mor, Inc.—to the outlandish, like purchasing a Boeing 737 jetliner for personal use—witness the creative expense accounts of Bill Agee and Mary Cunningham at the Knudsen Corporation.

A corporation exists to increase the wealth of its shareholders, who need designated speakers to protect them by voicing concerns should the actual people running the corporation abuse the rights of their fictitious charge. That's where directors come in.

Shareholders elect directors to be their voice and the voice of the corporation. Directors are accountable to them, monitor the corporation's officers and employees, and speak for the corporation in everything from annual reports to securities filings to strategic initiatives. Directors elect the officers of the corporation to manage it on a day-to-day basis. Those officers handle everything from employee compensation to the cafeteria contracts.

All corporations—profit and non-profit, private and public—must have a board to act as designated speaker on the corporation's legal, financial

> **Many of the good things that happen to companies and almost all of the bad things really emanate from the boardroom.**

Henry Wendt

and management issues. All states require a board of directors. But the number of directors required in each state varies. Under the Model Business Corporation Act, adopted in about one-third of the states, a corporation must have at least one board member. The structure and composition of the board are covered in Key 4.

In exchange for its legal existence and rights, a corporation has full liability for all of its contracts and actions. *All* corporate assets are on the line. But as long as the corporation operates properly with full regard for its rights as a fictitious person, its shareholders do not have to worry about personal liability for any of the corporation's unpaid obligations.

This limited liability is in jeopardy if the shareholders fail to treat the property and funds of a corporation as separate and subject to formalities including everything from approval of transactions to the annual filing of reports. The duty of formality belongs to the board of directors and those to whom they delegate responsibility. In effect, the board holds the responsibility to speak for the corporate person on behalf of the shareholders who elected its members.

The success and efficiency of corporations comes from a simple structure: shareholders vote for a board of directors, which delegates authority for day-to-day operations to a group of managers called officers (see Key 17). The board sets the course for the company and guides the officers as they carry out the board-charted course. The owners of a corporation may be widely dispersed but they retain their power through the ballot box. At the annual meeting where directors are elected, shareholders have the ultimate power to control both their investment and their designated agents, the directors of the board.

Should the board and its hired officers veer off the shareholders' desired course or continue along an ill-advised route, the shareholders have the power to replace the directors at the helm. Those new directors can then take the necessary steps to re-chart the course and, if necessary, use their power over officers to replace them. In short, shareholders—the ones with the money at risk—are supposed to rule.

How a board works and how well it speaks for its shareholders is a key component of a company's performance and financial success. Good fences make good neighbors and good boards make good returns on investments.

KEY 3

The board does a lot more than just collect a fee

In 1600, 218 English merchants formed the East India Company for the purpose of engaging in trade in the Far East. The first thing they did was set up a Court of Committees, 24 merchants who would serve to direct the affairs and investments of the world's first multinational corporation. By doing so, these merchants established the first board of directors. Boards are no different today. A board is the supervisor for the shareholders, a strategist, a protector and often, a rebel.

As a supervisor, the board is responsible for the recruiting, hiring, compensating and firing of officers. Those officers are then assigned the responsibility of managing the company with direction and input from the board. If the chief executive officer is not doing his job, or the chief financial officer is embezzling, it is the board's job to hand out the pink slips. General Motors' board stepped in when Robert Stempel was in charge and that Dustbuster-looking van was just one of many vehicles that was not selling. With losses mounting, GM's board ousted Mr. Stempel. The board of Sunbeam stepped in and, even without the use of weapons, managed to oust "Chainsaw" Al Dunlap as CEO when accounting irregularities and excess inventory led to unprecedented losses.

While the officer team manages day-to-day, a good board establishes the strategic plan for the company. Herman Miller moved from slumping sales in its $3,000 Eames executive chairs to growth built around much less expensive but still high quality modular office furniture after the board realized that the office furniture market was passing it by. Ben & Jerry's even moved away from management by Ben and Jerry when the board insisted on more experience in actually running a company.

The board's roles of protector and rebel often go hand-in-hand. Elected by the shareholders and accountable to them, the best directors are those who ask questions and challenge the officers they have hired. "Why do you do it that way?" "Why are you doing it at all?" During the late 1980's, IBM was losing ground in a market it had held for 25 years—several lifetimes in the fast moving computer business. With a change in management, the board was able to get what the shareholders needed for the protection of their investment: a redefinition of strategy for the company from a maker and seller of mainframe computers to the seller of computer systems, which offered total solutions for its customers. Such a repositioning required rebellion and a departure from what many asserted was IBM's identity in the computer market. The ouster of longstanding family officers and board members from Archer-Daniels-Midland after the company pleaded guilty to price-fixing charges is another example of a board cleaning house.

Norm Augustine, the chairman of Lockheed-Martin and a member of three boards, said that the best advice he was ever given as a board member was simple: "Always vote last and vote with the minority."

A checklist for a good board member who is a supervisor, strategist, rebel and protector follows:

◆ Come to meetings

◆ Come to meetings prepared, having reviewed the financials and background information

◆ Understand the industry and the mission of the company

◆ Be independent and have the ability to challenge management plans and assumptions

◆ Take nothing for granted

◆ Be ready to take action

Who picks the board members and why do they pick them?

Diversity, independence and experience are nearly always listed as important factors in the make-up of a corporate board. Some current data on corporate boards:

◆ In 1998, there were 671 women on the boards of Fortune 500 companies; women held 11% of the total board seats (6,064). Within the group, 86% had at least one female director. Those companies with the highest percentages of seats on the boards occupied by women included soap/cosmetics companies and banks; the lowest number of women served on boards in advertising firms.

◆ The typical corporate board has 12 members; 75% of the members are outsiders— those who are not officers of the company or affiliated with the company in some way.

◆ In 1998, 33% of the directors elected were CEOs of other companies; 19% were senior officers of the company itself; 12% were CFOs; 7% were retired CEOs; 7% were consultants; 6% were academics and 4% were lawyers.

♦ Blacks hold 2.3% of the directorships of Fortune 500 companies.

♦ Nearly half of Fortune 500 companies have ethnic minorities on their boards.

♦ Only 14% of Fortune 500 companies have a foreign representative on their boards.

Here's how a board member is typically selected: First, the chairman and/or the CEO or a nominating committee agree on a name or list of names. Second, those names are presented to the current board, perhaps with a visit from the prospective board members. Finally, the names of the proposed board members are placed on the annual proxy sent to the shareholders, who vote for the candidate or slate of candidates management presents.

The result of this process is the following profile of directors for Fortune 500 companies.

♦ Directors who represent major shareholders

♦ Traditional directors such as bankers and newspaper publishers

♦ Former government officials who are now directors

♦ Directors who are professionally involved with the corporation (lawyers, accountants)

♦ Directors with specialized expertise (marketing)

- Directors with general wisdom and sagacity

- Directors who are buddies of the CEO and/or chairman

Still, and here is where the great who-should-be-a-director debate starts to get interesting, not all shareholders, particularly institutional shareholders, are convinced that this buddy system of nomination and election necessarily nets the best candidates for the board. Is this the best way to insure independence and willingness to challenge the CEO and the management team? And is this the right way to pursue diversity?

Start with the issue of diversity. There is a certain amount of political correctness associated with the director selection process. Dorothea Brounder, an analyst at the Investor Responsibility Research Center has written, ". . . the center sees board inclusiveness as an issue of social justice as well as good business sense because the perpetuation of all-white-male boards may create feelings of hopelessness among those not represented and thereby may have an impact on society as a whole."

But there are practical reasons to pursue diversity. Some companies have been subject to shareholder proposals (see Key 22) requiring diversity and even possible consumer boycotts. For example, at Dr. Pepper/Seven Up, blacks account for 22% of the company's annual revenues and the company was threatened by the NAACP with a boycott if it did not place two blacks on its board, which the company did.

On the other hand, diversity does little to insure that the board carries out its principal responsibility, which is to protect the interests of the shareholders. T.J. Rodgers, the founder and CEO of Cypress Semiconductor was threatened by an order of nuns (the Sisters of St. Francis of Philadelphia) who wanted him to nominate a woman to the board. Mr. Rodgers responded:

Thank you for your letter criticizing the lack of racial and gender diversity of Cypress's Board of Directors. I received the same letter from you last year. I will reiterate the management arguments opposing your position. Then I will provide the philosophical basis behind our rejection of the operating principles espoused in your letter, which we believe to be not only unsound, but even immoral....

The semiconductor business is a tough one with significant competition from the Japanese, Taiwanese and Koreans. There have been more corporate casualties than survivors. For that reason, our Board of Directors is not a ceremonial watchdog, but a critical management function. The essential criteria for Cypress board membership are as follows:

Experience as a CEO of an important technology company

Direct expertise in the semiconductor business based on education and management experience

Direct experience in the management of a company that buys from the semi-conductor industry

A search based on these criteria usually yields a male who is 50-plus years old, has a Master's degree in engineering science and has moved up the managerial ladder to the top spot in one or more corporations. Unfortunately, there are currently few minorities and almost no women who chose to be engineering graduate students 30 years ago (this picture will be dramatically different in

10 years, due to the greater diversification of graduate students in the 80's). Bluntly stated, a "woman's view" on how to run our semiconductor company does not help us, unless that woman has an advanced technical degree and experience as a CEO. I do realize there are other industries in which the last statement does not hold true. We would quickly embrace the opportunity to include any woman or minority person who could help us as a director, because we pursue talent and we don't care in what package that talent comes.

I believe that placing arbitrary racial or gender quotas on corporate boards is fundamentally wrong.

And then there is the Warren Buffett model for corporate boards: six members, three of whom are Mr. Buffett, his wife and son. Mr. Buffett's vice chairman is a fourth member and Mr. Buffett begrudgingly added two independent members when Berkshire Hathaway listed its stock on the New York Stock Exchange, which requires at least two independent directors. Few can argue that the Warren Buffett model has hampered the increase of shareholder wealth.

These are testy times for selecting directors. And because the public and the media, not just investors, are now involved, the task of searching for and nominating directors is unlikely to get any easier. One manager for an institutional investor, when asked why he did not submit candidates for board membership in the companies in which his firm held interests replied, "You'll never get me sticking my neck out like that."

Perhaps the best approach in picking a candidate for board membership is the most obvious but not always the most common: ignore both the demands of political correctness and the buddy system and actually look for those who are best qualified. Paul Ray, a director at Georgia-Pacific Corporation and chairman of an international search firm described an ideal director as follows: "It's not enough for a candidate to simply represent diversity. There must be a solid record of accomplishment for a candidate to be taken seriously. An executive must have first-class credentials and deep knowledge of the industry or industries in which she's worked. Further, she should be battle-tested. She needs to demonstrate that she's grappled with the sorts of issues she's likely to face as a director."

The following traits are desirable for directors:

◆ Business experience, which may include related experience or experience in an area in which the company needs help. For example, an electric utility might place a phone company executive on its board to help navigate its coming deregulation since telephone companies have already gone through the experience.

◆ Knowledge of the company or industry

◆ Integrity

◆ Ability to make the time commitment to serving on the board

◆ Limited insider relationships and contacts, if any

The benefit of these criteria is that they provide sound business justification for board composition. No one ever disputes qualified candidates.

The beef with boards lies with the choice of friends, relatives and others unlikely to question the CEO. Why have a board at all if the CEO always gets his way unchallenged and unquestioned?

We directors all looked alike, dressed alike, talked alike, and enjoyed each other's company.
And one after another, the companies got into trouble.
How come?

Stanley Foster Reed

Electing board members is still the shareholder's job

Shareholders elect directors, CEOs don't. The power of shareholders is wielded at the annual meetings where elections for directors are held. Under the Model Business Corporation Act, if, for any reason, the annual meeting has not been held in 15 months, shareholders can demand such a meeting.

Every shareholder who owns voting shares in a corporation has the right to cast votes for director candidates listed on the proxy, which includes timely notice of the annual meeting along with information and materials required under state and federal laws.

The proxy must be sent to each shareholder. The information in the proxy includes:

◆ Names and brief background information for director nominees

◆ Issues management wants shareholders to

act on, (e.g., changes in articles of incorporation or any major transactions such as mergers)

- Any shareholder proposals (see Key 22) for shareholder vote

- Required statutory information on the compensation of the top five officers as well as financial performance information so that shareholders can compare salaries of officers with results.

- The shareholders are given this information before casting their vote or they can sign the proxy form included in the proxy materials and designate another to vote for them.

The era when shareholders signed away their proxies by endorsing their dividend checks is long gone. Shareholders have full information before they vote. Under the 1934 Securities Exchange Act (Section 14), the proxy materials must be approved by the Securities and Exchange Commission (SEC) before they are sent to shareholders. If the materials are not sent out prior to the vote at the meeting, the SEC can set aside the action taken at the meeting. Regulation of proxy solicitation is not limited to corporate management; shareholders seeking a vote on any issue must also garner the SEC's approval prior to proxy solicitation.

The actual voting process is usually one share = one vote. Some companies provide for cumulative voting in their articles of incorporation. Under cumulative voting, if a shareholder owns, say, 100 shares and there are 9 directors to be elected, the shareholder gets 900 votes. The idea behind cumulative voting is to give minority shareholders a greater chance to make their voices heard by concentrating their votes on a single candidate or a small number of candidates.

Voting one's shares need not be a completely independent process and shareholders can wield power through organizing their votes. Some shareholders create a voting trust, transferring their shares to a trust. A trustee votes their shares according to the terms of the trust agreement. The shareholders in the trust no longer hold their shares but the trust certificate entitles them to all the rights of a shareholder, including dividends— except the right to vote. A copy of the voting trust must be filed with the secretary of the corporation or with the officer responsible for the notices, proxies and votes at the annual meeting.

Pooling agreements are also used by share-holders. A pooling agreement is simply a contract to vote a certain way, such as casting all your votes as a shareholder for a particular candidate for the board. A pooling agreement is a contract, but the problem is enforcing it. If a shareholder disregards the terms of his pooling agreement, his vote still counts as cast and there is no reversing the corporate action once taken. In situations where the pooled votes would not have made a difference in outcome, it is nearly impossible to establish damages for breach of pooling contract.

At the annual meeting, the secretary of the corporation is generally responsible for the determination that a quorum of shareholders is present in person or by proxy. The secretary also tabulates the votes along with election inspectors appointed prior to the annual meeting. There are generally at least two election inspectors—one representing shareholders. This process is designed to insure that shareholders always have access to the ballot box as a remedy to keep the board of directors in line.

> **The directors of such companies, being the managers rather of other people's money than their own, it cannot well be expected that they would watch over it with the same anxious vigilance with which the partners in a private copartnery frequently watch their own.**

Adam Smith

KEY 6

Tenure for directors is not a good idea

How long should board members serve? In 1997, CalPERS, the huge California pension fund and perhaps the most active institutional investor bent on board reform, proposed that directors should serve no longer than 10 years. There was sufficient yipping and hollering by board members and shareholders alike that the proposal was withdrawn, but the issue remains a sensitive and critical one.

The real challenge is how to insure an effective board. Some subscribe to the theory that new blood is continually necessary for the company and its management team to keep pace with a rapidly changing world. Others argue that a seasoned board member can prove invaluable so long as he continues to recognize important issues and raises them in meetings and with the senior management team.

Controlling tenure on boards is easier when the board is divided into classes of directors and their election terms are staggered. A nine member board, for example, divided into three staggered classes of three directors each, means that just one-third of the directors are up for election each year. In the glaring light of annual meeting, the performance of three directors is much more likely to be addressed than a lost-among-the-masses non-performer.

Some companies have established limits in their by-laws on director tenure. Some have mandatory retirement ages and others impose a 15-year maximum for service.

Other corporations, however, are working against getting rid of directors who don't perform by affording them retirement plans. In 1995, 30 Fortune 500 companies had shareholder proposals challenging pension plans for directors. The question the shareholders raise in the proposals is the wisdom of affording directors benefits not tied in some way to the corporation's performance. Directors paid in stock have motivation to keep that stock price high. Directors paid in cash get paid even when the stock dives. Directors with a vested interest in a retirement plan of the company may behave differently. Guaranteed compensation for those in charge of the company's fate does not sit well with shareholders who must endure the slings and arrows of an often-unforgiving investment community. For example, a proposal by Philip Morris shareholders noted that such director pension plans are "management's way to ensure their directors unquestioning loyalty and acquiescence to whatever policy management initiates. Accordingly, when viewed from this perspective, these types of retirement benefits become yet another device to enhance and entrench management's control over corporate policy while being accountable only to themselves and not the company's owners." A shareholder proposal aimed at McGraw-Hill referred to such plans as "cronyism."

Many companies, though, have changed their methods of compensating directors (see Key 7) so that remuneration is tied to results and is not an automatic reward for board service.

The clear message in all shareholder activism regarding directors is quality: is this director still making a contribution and does this director take her responsibility seriously? While many of the proposals and by-laws address stagnation ineffectively, no director should ever assume a directorship lasts forever, or even to retirement.

Compensation in theory and practice: do directors deserve what they earn?

eave it to corporate management to develop a payment plan for directors even more complex than the union scale for the Screen Actor's Guild. Consider the types of fees found in Fortune 500 companies:

Retainers. These are annual fees paid to directors regardless of what they do—even if they do nothing. Retainer fees could be called the price a corporation pays to someone like Vernon Jordan for the right to associate its name with his. Henry Kissinger, Laura Tyson, the former chief economic adviser to President Bill Clinton, and George Mitchell, the former Senator, to name just a few, don't come cheap. In 1998, annual retainers ranged from $7,000 to $100,000.

Meeting Fees. These are the fees directors are paid to attend board and committee meetings. If you pay them, the theory goes, they will come. How do you get a big name you have retained to actually come to your board meetings? You pay them enough to make it worthwhile. Fees for meetings range from $100 to $7,000. And some companies trade off. They have lower retainers but pay well for meetings. Some companies vary their meeting fees—the fee for a board meeting is higher than the fee for a committee meeting. Some even pay more for a committee meeting held on a different day from the regular board meeting.

Payment in shares. This type of compensation is viewed as an incentive plan for directors. The more shares you own, the more you will pay attention to running the company well. The better the company does and the higher its share price goes, the better your compensation.

Performance-based stock options. At SYSCO, Inc., an international food distributor, and Dun and Bradstreet, directors are given share options based on performance targets. Referred to as performance shares, directors can obtain up to 1,000 share options if the company reaches a certain level of performance, for example, matching the 50th percentile of the S&P 500 returns. If the company comes in beneath the target, the directors may get nothing or or only a percentage of the potential grant.

Pension and retirement plans. This form of compensation, which has raised a ruckus among many shareholder activists, is often labeled an inherent conflict of interest as well as a problem when it comes to getting directors to leave.

Charitable contributions. Some companies agree to make an annual charitable contribution to a director's favorite non-profit organization. Others provide a contribution upon the director's death, which is often paid out of the proceeds of a life insurance policy paid for by the company.

Deferred compensation plans. Some companies permit directors to defer their compensation through a modified 401(k) plan. Directors can defer their fees until after their retirement from their own jobs.

Consulting fees. Henry Kissinger earned them from American Express while serving on its board. If the consulting fees truly are for work performed for the company, then, at certain levels, there must be public disclosure. Consulting fees create an inherent conflict of interest, though, meaning that the recipient no longer qualifies as an independent director. The level and type of compensation for directors continues to be a sensitive issue with shareholders and, as a result, a sensitive issue with managers. Reform suggestions include elimination of the cash-only retainer fee in exchange for stock equivalents. Many experts believe that 50% cash and 50% stock in the company is a good mix. Some suggest eliminating meeting fees, making up for the loss through a more generous annual retainer. There are also many recommendations for reducing the complexity of board compensation. Most experts agree that consulting fees for directors should be eliminated altogether as a conflict of interest.

Pink slips for directors

Sacking a director is never easy. But some moves are worse than others. For example, H. Ross Perot became a director at General Motors after G.M. acquired his company and he became one of the largest shareholders. But Mr. Perot's down-home criticism, usually issued along the lines of "Now, looky here. You aren't runnin' this bidness right," didn't go down well with the buttoned-down bureaucrats at G.M. G.M. was forced to borrow heavily to buy Mr. Perot's shares to make him go away.

Directors are removed because of philosophical differences, as in the G.M./Perot case. They are removed due to lackluster performance, as when there is a failure to attend meetings. And they are often removed when there is a significant change in share ownership, such as a merger or takeover. Occasionally, a director is the subject of nasty litigation in securities law or develops a conflict of interest in terms of other professional obligations and the removal is necessary by law.

How does one get rid of a director? Under the MBCA, a director can be removed with or without cause so long as the proper procedures are followed. One way is for the board to adopt a resolution, which is often tough to come by because it means that the directors are going to sit together in a room and vote to give one of their colleagues the heave-ho. That resolution is then placed before the shareholders for a vote.

More likely, there will be insurrection among shareholders demanding a special meeting to vote on a director or directors. Of course, shareholders can always vote out a director at an annual meeting. The problem is corporations don't have write-in ballots so the removal of directors and replacement is a two-step process for which shareholders are not well prepared or organized.

Whether by resolution or rebellion, the shareholders end up voting on removal. But the process is always messy and tends to hurt the stock. And it is distracting for management.

That's why most directors are removed informally: the CEO pays a visit or makes a call and asks for the director's resignation quietly. It is explained as a voluntary move, leaving the slot open for a replacement. While the burden for removal usually falls upon the chairman of the board or the CEO, such actions are often instigated by other board members. The problem is solved, face is saved, and shareholders satisfied as the board handles the tension in the air with its private call for a director's resignation.

Directors' fiduciary duty:
it's not their money

Fiduciary is a legal term used to label those who assume a position of responsibility for others or their property. The law imposes its highest degree of care and responsibility on fiduciaries. A trustee of a trust is a fiduciary. A lawyer is a fiduciary to his or her client. The executor of an estate is a fiduciary. A fiduciary puts the interests of another party above his own interests. A fiduciary never profits from the fiduciary relationship. A fiduciary does not withhold information nor use proprietary information. In short, a fiduciary must be beyond reproach with a stellar record of selflessness with respect to the fiduciary relationship. A fiduciary makes the rest of us ill with his exemplary ethics but that doesn't stop us from being grateful for fiduciaries when it comes to watching over our money.

Directors are fiduciaries for corporations and their shareholders. Directors must act in the best interests of the corporation on whose board they serve. They are not supposed to use their position for self-serving conduct. But that sometimes happens.

For example, many years ago when a company called Loft's grew resentful over the high prices Coca-Cola charged for supplying fountain syrup for its stores, one of its owners/directors/officers, Charles G. Guth, began to pursue an alternative. In this pursuit, Mr. Guth found the corporation holding the secret formula and trademark for Pepsi-Cola in bankruptcy. Grace Company and Guth's family syrup business purchased the bankrupt Pepsi-Cola together.

Mr. Guth then proceeded to use Loft's working capital, its plant and equipment and its credit to produce Pepsi-Cola. Loft became Pepsi-Cola's chief customer for fountain syrup and Loft dropped Coca-Cola as a supplier like a hot potato. Loft, however, lost customers who preferred Coca-Cola, so Mr. Guth began using Loft's funds to advertise Pepsi. The advertising paid off, and the rest, as they say is history.

The board of Loft, however, suddenly took notice and felt Loft's should have been given the right to buy Pepsi. And the Delaware court of Chancery agreed and, in no uncertain terms, chastised Mr. Guth:

> Guth took without limit or stint from a helpless corporation, in violation of a statute enacted for the protection of corporations against such abuses, and without the knowledge or authority of the corporation's Board of Directors. Cunning and craft supplanted sincerity. Frankness gave way to concealment. He did not offer the Pepsi-Cola opportunity to Loft, but captured it for himself. He invested little or no money of his own in the

venture, but commandeered for his own benefit and advantage the money, resources and facilities of his corporation and the services of his officials. He thrust upon Loft the hazard, while he reaped the benefit. His time was paid for by Loft. The use of the Grace plant was not essential to the enterprise. In such manner he acquired for himself and Grace ninety-one percent of the capital stock of Pepsi-Cola, now worth many millions. A genius in his line he may be, but the law makes no distinction between the wrongdoing genius and the one less endowed.

This was one unhappy court and one humbled director. Owners/directors/officers cannot make profits for themselves while using corporate facilities and resources. The Pepsi profits belonged to Loft's because of Mr. Guth's breach of fiduciary duty.

Fiduciaries watch out for others who can't be there to supervise. Whether serving as a trustee for an estate when the decedent has departed or as a director for shareholders who can't be there each day to watch over the use of their money, a fiduciary works to protect the interests of others rather than his own. Fiduciaries are supposed to be near perfect in their conduct and are held accountable and liable when that perfection slips.

In addition to their role as fiduciaries, directors face some additional obligations: exercising good business judgment, not seizing an opportunity from company for their own profit, watching carefully for conflicts in their work with the board and the like. The next 10 keys describe these director-specific duties.

Mistakes or errors of judgment?

Directors make mistakes. They are permitted certain types and levels of mistakes under the legal principle called the business judgment rule. The business judgment rule means simply that courts will not substitute their business judgment *ex post facto* for the judgment of the board at the time it made its business decision. No judicial second-guessing of directors is permitted.

For example, in 1968, shareholders of the Chicago Cubs organization were sufficiently irritated to file suit against the Cubs' board for its consistent refusal to allow night games at Wrigley Field. All other 19 teams in the National League at that time played night games. The shareholders argued that the board was passing up a lucrative source of revenues. The board responded that night games would increase the safety risk and threaten the character of the neighborhood and alter the tradition of the Cubs.

Under the liability limitation protections of the

I don't believe I could have known, therefore I don't believe I should have known.

Walter Forbes

business judgment rule, the court ruled in favor of the Cubs' directors. The board may have been wrong, the court said, but they did have their reasons for being wrong.

The business judgment rule does have some limitations in its protection. Slacker directors do not enjoy immunity: They are required to give the time and effort necessary to make a reasonable business judgment. If directors do their homework and attend meetings and make a mistake, the business judgment rule affords them protection. If they miss meetings and are not prepared and then make a mistake, they cannot invoke the business judgment rule. Courts are really quite testy when directors don't do their homework and miss class, so to speak. If a director researches an issue, reads the materials, and attends meetings and still makes a mistake, there is protection. Directors who let other directors do their work by not attending meetings and by being an inactive board member will find themselves on the line when their colleagues make a bad business judgment.

Other types of conduct that will cost directors the protection of the business judgment rule include the failure to obtain outside advice on critical issues. For example, in a case in which the senior management of TransUnion Corporation had proposed a merger with another company the directors met only briefly, took management's assertions, reports and data as fact and did not request any outside evaluation of the proposed merger. Based on a 20-minute oral presentation by the chairman, the directors approved the merger in less than two hours. The directors did not have an accurate figure on the per share value of the company. A shareholder filed suit and the court found the TransUnion directors could not invoke the business judgment rule because the premise of the rule is that the directors have made a reasoned, tempered and supportable decision. They can be wrong and not liable. But directors cannot be wrong and careless or precipitous and expect to escape liability.

For the protection from liability the business judgment rule provides, directors must:

◆ Attend meetings

◆ Prepare for meetings

◆ Obtain independent advice beyond management

◆ Deliberate carefully, often requiring more than one meeting for a decision

Carpe diem, *but not the opportunity*

Because directors are fiduciaries, they are not permitted to capitalize on business opportunities that come their way that might interest the corporation. For example, a director on the board of Scott Paper would need to share with the board of Scott an opportunity for acquisition of land for logging. As explained in Key 9, Loft's had the right to look at Pepsi as a business opportunity before one of its directors, Charles Guth, took it for his own.

But the results of following that rule are not always beneficial to the company. Former Arizona governor J. Fife Symington used the corporate opportunity doctrine in his defense in a savings and loan case. Southwest Savings loaned money to the governor's development firm (a business he ran before being elected) while the governor was a member of the Southwest Savings & Loan board. Allegations of conflict of interest were raised about Mr. Symington's dual role as debtor and board member. But Mr. Symington defended himself successfully on the grounds that as a director of Southwest he had a responsibility to present the loan opportunity to the board of Southwest before taking it elsewhere. That the loans went bad did not mean they were not a corporate opportunity at the outset. Mr. Symington argued persuasively that the failure to present the opportunity for the loans to his development company to the Southwest Savings board would have been a violation on his part of the corporate opportunity doctrine.

When a director is presented with an opportunity related to the corporation's business, the director must take three steps:

- The opportunity must be presented to the board.

- The board must affirmatively reject the opportunity. ("Affirmatively reject" sounds like doublespeak but simply means that the board actually takes action to reject the opportunity rather than just tabling the issue.)

- The director must indicate his or her intent to take the opportunity.

If the director does not take these three steps, then any profits the director makes pursuing the opportunity belong to the corporation. A corporate opportunity belongs first of all to the corporation and not to its directors.

KEY 12

Conflicts, contracts and independent directors

A board member represents the shareholders in a corporation. Directors' decisions must be made in the best interests of the company, not their own or that of management.

Directors with a vested interest in pleasing management tend to focus on personal gains or business retention. A lawyer whose firm earns, say, one-sixth of its revenue performing services for a corporation will not be an independent director on that corporation's board. Because her firm's contract with the company and resulting revenues are contingent upon satisfying the company's officers who arrange for the legal services, the lawyer/board member would have a conflict between what's best for the shareholders and what senior management desires.

The same types of conflicts arise when an officer from a corporation's major supplier agrees to sit on the board. The fiduciary duty of the director is in conflict with his vested financial interest. A banker on the board may be more willing to approve financial statements for the company that really should be qualified. After all, he may be more worried about having the loan repaid than informing shareholders that the company is in trouble.

Conflicts like these incestuous business interconnections are complex, and they don't necessarily rule out serving on a board. But directors need to be careful to watch out for all types of conflicts, many of which at least merit disclosure or perhaps an abstention from a vote.

For example, a director may serve on the board of a bank and also on the board of a utility. If the board of the utility votes on a credit line arrangement with the bank, the director who serves on both boards is in conflict. She should abstain from voting on the credit line, disclose her interest in the bank, and have the secretary for the corporation put a note in the minutes reflecting the disclosure and abstention from voting. The same is true for a director who happens to be a major shareholder in the bank offering the line of credit.

Conflicts for board members as they seek to exercise their fiduciary responsibilities fall into the following general categories:

♦ The director has a financial interest in contracts with the corporation (supplier, law firm). The desire to retain business is in conflict with the best interests of the corporation.

♦ The director sits on the board or is a large shareholder of another company and that company will benefit from approval of a contract with a firm on whose board he also sits.

- ◆ The director has family beneficiaries of corporate contracts; for instance, the corporation is doing business with a company owned by his wife.

- ◆ The corporation is making substantial charitable contributions to an organization run by the director's spouse.

The best advice for directors in avoiding conflicts is ADQ: abstain, disclose and always question your ability to be independent in those circumstances where your firm and the firm you are asked to serve on have conflicting interests. Remember, the conflict exists whether or not you are influenced by the different interests.

On being sued: directors' liability and insurance

The business judgment rule described earlier provides some protection for directors. But the complexities of corporate life and law mean that directors still may easily end up as defendants in litigation. Even if they emerge victorious, the cost of mounting a legal defense can be prohibitive.

To cover these litigation costs for directors, corporations are authorized to carry what is commonly referred to "D & O" insurance. D is for director and O is for officer and the two letters together mean that directors and officers get insurance coverage when they are sued by shareholders for certain types of conduct. The conduct not covered under a D & O policy is covered in Key 14. The conduct covered under a D & O policy includes everything from negligence on the part of directors and officers to violations of environmental laws.

Directors have been sued for the acquisition of a company that later failed as well as the failure to diversify. If the books of a company are cooked, the directors and officers may be sued for the failure to provide adequate internal controls and supervision. In the *In re Caremark* case, a landmark decision on director liability, the court held that the failure of a board to establish adequate checks and balances for corporate spending and bookkeeping is a breach of a director's fiduciary duty. Not minding the store is a basis for director liability which is covered under D & O.

D & O insurance is purchased by the company and covers directors, officers and, especially in employment litigation, other employees of the company acting at the direction of officers and directors. The amount of coverage carried depends upon the nature of the company and its line of business. Directors serving on a utility with a nuclear plant simply cannot get too much D & O coverage. Few companies would carry policies for less than $100 million because verdicts and settlements of that size are not at all unusual.

For the most part, D & O insurance protects directors when shareholders challenge a decision. And shareholders have become increasingly active litigators.

Indeed, when Congress passed the Securities Litigation Reform Act in 1998, one of the act's provisions required that shareholders actually be aware that they have filed a suit before the suit can be filed. Apparently suits were being brought by lawyers who knew D & O coverage would kick in, but these lawyers forgot to notify the plaintiffs they were allegedly representing that they were indeed bringing suit against a corporation in which they held shares. In short, the litigation against directors and officers had gotten a little out of hand. While the new law was intended to curb litigation against directors and officers, its impact has been minimal and D & O insurance is as necessary as ever.

In addition to litigation and liability over corporate decisions, directors and officers may find that their greatest exposure lies in employment practices liability (EPL). Claims against companies for employment practices are frequent and costly. Texaco settled a race discrimination charge for over $100 million. So did Shoney's. State Farm settled an expensive gender discrimination case. As of this writing, Coca-Cola faces a race discrimination class action lawsuit for discrimination in its evaluation process for white-collar workers (Coke has filed a motion to dismiss the case). The size of the settlements in these cases demands high levels of coverage. A $100 million employment practices case can exhaust a company's D & O coverage.

As a result, many companies now carry a separate EPL policy, or a stand-alone policy. In addition to protection for directors and officers, these EPL policies also provide coverage for the corporation. One expert has noted that carrying only D & O coverage for EPL is like insuring the contents of your house against fire but not the house itself. A separate EPL policy can also include coverage for punitive damages, since some of the awards in such cases could break a bank, let alone a textile company.

A board should review the D & O coverage each year to be certain that the amounts are adequate, that it covers all expected types of risks and that the insurer can be counted on to pay off. There are plenty of off-shore D & O insurers. But if one of them refuses to pay, good luck trying to enforce your contract. Directors should be certain that they have early coverage, plenty of it, and extensive protection against all kinds of risks.

On being sued personally: directors without insurance

There are some types of conduct by directors that all the D & O insurance in the world will not cover because D & O insurers have been smart enough to exclude it. Basically, directors will not be covered by insurance if they engage in conduct that is intentionally bad or dishonest. For example, Phar-Mor, Inc. experienced all sort of setbacks, including a Chapter 11 bankruptcy, when it was discovered that the company was keeping two sets of books. Insiders called one set of books the "cookies." The other was called "cookies with raisins." The cookies with raisins was the accurate set of books.

The reason for the two varieties of cookies was simple. Michael Monus, the former president and a director who has since been sentenced to prison, was funneling corporate funds to his pet project, the World Basketball League, an alternative league for "short" players in which all the players are 6'7" or under. Directors are held personally liable for their conduct when they are embezzling. Who wants to insure an embezzler?

Other types of conduct not covered by D & O insurance include securities fraud, check kiting, RICO violations (racketeering), price fixing and other intentional antitrust activities, and bribery. In other words, criminal conduct is not covered by D & O insurance. In those situations, directors and officers are not only on their own for their own criminal defense, they are on their own when shareholder suits come rolling in against them. Corporations don't indemnify directors for criminal conduct and D & O policies do not cover directors in shareholder suits based on criminal conduct.

In addition to the criminal types of conduct excluded from coverage, D & O policies may place limitations on coverage. For example, some policies will not cover certain environmental liabilities. If the company learns that it sits upon a site with a great deal of hazardous, but buried, waste and the clean-up will by costly, shareholders may bring suit because such an announcement is bound to bring the stock price down. But some policies specifically exclude environmental liability issues because they are such a great unknown and because the costs of clean up can be so extensive. Many corporations' regular insurance policies exclude coverage for such environmental clean-up liabilities. Special riders for coverage of such environmental liabilities can be purchased.

As managers of a company's pension plan, directors also have extensive liability for missteps. Boards may carry additional coverage or separate riders for the management of pension plans. While directors can hire help to assist them in pension fund management, they cannot delegate the duty away.

There are other types of conduct for which directors and officers are held personally liable and for which there is no D & O coverage. Those include the failure to pay wage taxes.

Sexual harassment is another common area of litigation. A suit against a company may be covered under an EPL rider or policy. But an individual director or officer found liable for personal sexual harassment would not be covered under the D & O policy. That's an area of personal liability that no officer or director can escape.

Federal laws and criminal sanctions: the SEC and other things that can go bump in the boardroom

Apart from IRS, the most important initials that every director should keep in mind are SEC. The SEC is the Securities and Exchange Commission; It is the federal agency responsible for the oversight of the sales of securities and the stock markets. SEC regulation affects every director and every boardroom.

There are two statutes under which the SEC regulates securities and markets.

The first is the 1933 Securities Act, which provides the regulatory framework for the issuance of securities by corporations. Whether an offering is an initial public offering or one of many other types of methods of raising money, the SEC requires that the securities be registered prior to sale unless the securities being offered qualify for for an exemption. Every member of the board is required to sign those registration papers. Put your signature on a SEC document and you have liability. If the registration materials turn out to be false or misleading, or important information is knowingly omitted, the company and its directors face both criminal and civil liability.

For example, in *Escott v. BarChris Industries, Inc.*, a company that built and operated bowling alleys overstated its income, its assets, its alleys in operation and understated its debt in financial statements filed with the SEC for the issuance of bonds needed to raise capital for expansion and construction. All of the officers and directors who signed the registration statement for the bonds were held liable when the company's bowling alley expansion plan collapsed. One director had been made a director only a few days before his signed the registration statement. He tried the "I just came on the board" defense, but the judge was unmoved. The judge warned that no director should sign "something for the SEC," as the new director phrased it, without first asking a few questions.

The second statute regulating markets and securities in the 1934 Securities Exchange Act. This statute imposes mandatory reporting requirements on companies that trade on national exchanges or reach a certain size. These include quarterly financial reports (10Q's), annual financial reports (10K's) and monthly updates on changes in the company's status (8K's).

The 1934 Act also includes protections for investors in the marketplace against directors who might wield too much power in that market based on information gleaned from their position. Among these protections are those commonly referred to as the sanctions against insider trading, which are covered in Key 16. But there are other provisions in the 1934 Act that bear on directors and officers owning and trading shares in their own companies.

Under Section 16 of the Act, officers, directors and holders of more than 10 percent of the company's shares must file a disclosure statement indicating that status in the month in which they become an officer, director or 10 percent shareholder. The second part of Section 16 regulates short-term profits by such individuals. No officer, director or 10 percent shareholder can make a gain through a trade that takes place in less than six months. The following example illustrates:

May 1, 1999	Director buys 100 shares for $10 each
June 15, 1999	Director sells 100 shares for $6 each
July 22, 1999	Director buys 100 shares for $4 each

The SEC matches the highest sale with the lowest purchase in any six-month period. If there is a profit, the director, officer or 10 percent shareholder owes that profit back to the corporation. In this scenario, the director has a $200 profit because the highest sale is at $6 per share and the lowest purchase is at $4 per share. The SEC does not net out transactions because the purpose of Section 16 is to impose a six-month holding period on those who have ready access to the company's financial information. Section 16's profit rules apply regardless of whether the director, officer or 10 percent shareholder possessed sensitive information at the time of the stock transactions. The watchword for directors is long-term profits.

Inside information:
the law on juicy tidbits

Federal securities laws consider all directors to be insiders, meaning that they have access to information about their companies that is not generally available to the market. Under Section 10(b) of the 1934 Securities Exchange Act, directors cannot trade on inside information. For example, a director will know long before the information becomes public that a merger of his company with another company is in the works. Generally the announcement that a company is about to be acquired sends the stock price higher. But insiders are not permitted to profit from that information by buying stock in advance of the announcement. Trading on inside information is a felony. Any profits that an insider makes trading on such information will be turned over to the SEC and/or the persons from whom those profits were made.

When the regulation of insider trading was first promulgated, some people thought that perhaps they could avoid insider trading sanctions by simply passing the information along to others and allowing these non-insiders to trade. Such persons, while not insiders, are still subject to 10(b) because they got their information from insiders. For example, Mervyn Cooper, a psychotherapist, happened to be treating a Lockheed executive in a troubled marriage while the executive was working on the Lockheed merger with Martin Marietta. In fact, the pressure the executive felt with the work on the merger came up during the counseling session. Dr. Cooper passed the information along to a friend, Kenneth Rottenberg, who then proceeded to buy options on Lockheed stock for the two of them. Mr. Rottenberg, warned by his broker about the risks of call options, assured the broker that a major announcement was coming, disclosing that he had inside information. Both Dr. Cooper and Mr. Rottenberg were charged by the SEC with violations of 10(b) and paid back their profits of nearly $200,000 along with a fine equivalent to those profits.

While the statute is clear that insiders and so-called "tippees" are covered under the insider trading sanctions, the definitions remain a bit muddled. A live-in boyfriend tipped by his lover that her company has just landed a big government contract cannot trade on her company's stock prior to the public announcement. But a patron in a theater lobby who overhears a discussion between that same couple out celebrating her success in landing the contract could go ahead and trade on the stock.

But while the definition of who is an insider may be muddled, one thing remains consistently clear: directors are always insiders and cannot profit in advance from their company's plans. Directors must wait until information becomes public to trade in their company's stock. In fact, most companies have hard and fast rules on insider trading by directors and officers. During so-called "blackout" periods, directors and officers are not permitted to do any trading in the company's stock. These periods tend to be those just prior to the release of monthly or quarterly financial statements. During window periods, there is a safe harbor for trading and these periods tend to follow immediately the company's public announcements or release of earnings. Even during window periods, many companies require directors to check with the company's legal counsel before trading in the stock.

One final aspect of insider trading rules is the obligation of the officers and directors to be forthcoming about the company's status and any changes. Information released to the public should be neither overly optimistic nor overly pessimistic. For example, in one of the landmark cases on information and corporate disclosure, *SEC v. Texas Gulf Sulphur*, the company released overly pessimistic information about a mineral find. While the market digested that negative information, directors and officers traded on the company's stock and then announced that, indeed, the mineral find was the largest in its history. The directors and officers had violated 10(b) in their release of misleading information and then further violated it by trading on that misleading information's effect on the price of their company's stock in the market.

The penalties for insider trading include civil and criminal penalties. The criminal charges carry up to five years in prison. The public disgrace can last a lot longer.

KEY 17

Who's in charge here?

The sharcholders elect the board and the board elects the officers. The number of officers required in a corporation varies from state-to-state but there must generally be an officer in charge, usually the president and/or the CFO, and another officer designated as the keeper of corporate records.

The most common officer positions are chief executive officer (CEO), chief operating officer (COO), chief financial officer (CFO), and vice presidents for human resources and marketing. Nearly all corporations have a vice presidential level position for their general counsel, who may also serve as the corporate secretary, the most common position designated for keeping the corporate records. Newer types of officer-level positions include vice president for environmental, ethics or compliance officer and chief information officer (CIO).

These days, positions at the officer level are gen-

That's my gut feel. Now I'll recognize any other guts.

Harvard Business Review

erally recruited via executive search firms. Existing officers of the company then engage in initial interviews. Candidates for the position could include employees from inside the company, or those contacted at other companies by the search firm. The board makes the ultimate decision about hiring officers and may also conduct interviews in making that decision. The board's decision is made in a formal fashion with nomination, discussion and vote.

As part of the discussion and vote, the board will reach a decision on compensation. Officers are generally paid a base salary that varies significantly from industry to industry. But to enjoy the protection of the business judgment rule, directors should hire compensation consultants to run comparisons and offer suggestions on keeping salaries competitive. Officers are usually also paid bonuses or additional salary based on an incentive plan. Compensation in company stock has become a very popular form of officer pay. The theory is to compensate the officer in a way so that his interests are tied closely to that of the general shareholder. For example, Warren Buffett accepted only $100,000 as chairman of Berkshire Hathaway because he believes in drawing his compensation from the increase in the value of the company's shares.

There are few issues that have caused greater shareholder dissent and contention than the issue of compensation.

Compensation of at least the top five officers must be disclosed each year and the proxy solicitation for the annual meeting must include a chart on the corporation's financial performance so that shareholders can see if they are getting results from the officers for the compensation paid.

The levels of compensation have become a contentious shareholder issue and have been challenged at a number of corporate shareholder meetings. In 1998, Sanford Weill, the co-CEO of Citigroup, received $141.6 million in direct compensation for his officer role in the company. Other highly paid CEO's that year included L. Dennis Kozlowski of Tyco International at $74.4 million, Jack Welch of General Electric at $52.8 million and Sumner Redstone of Viacom at $50.5 million.

Some efforts, such as the federal regulation setting a limit of $1 million on the deductibility of executive salaries, are little more than public relations moves. They have done nothing to slow the increase in executive pay.

Milton Friedman, the Nobel Prize winning economist and well-known advocate of free-market solutions to most problems, thinks corporate governance is the right way to address salary issues. If shareholders think officers are being paid too much, the proper remedy is to remove the directors and vote in new ones. While board members hire and fire officers and set their salaries, shareholders hire and fire board members and can exercise indirect control.

Michael S. Kesner, National Director of Compensation and Benefits for Arthur Andersen Company has made the following observation about officer compensation:

> With restructuring, cost-cutting, and consolidation the order of the day, the actual impact of, say a $5 million CEO package on the bottom line of a $2 billion sales company is not clearly the issue. People are now saying, to paraphrase the sound advice of late Illinois Senator Everett Dirksen, "Hey, a percent of a billion here and a percent of a billion there adds up to real money." In light of widespread plant closings, layoffs, and long lines of unemployed workers seeking limited jobs, "pay for performance" has simply taken a backseat to what the general public considers "fair." As a result, the issue has moved from the business arena to the political arena. Corporate compensation levels have become only one target in a growing populist movement against public figures who have been afforded undue privileges. The effect of this should be apparent to all: individuals in both the public and private sectors are now opting to repudiate or reduce those privileges. This self-regulation ought to be encouraged.

The direct approach to self-regulation is through the board and its compensation plan for officers.

Board committees:
extra fees or real purpose?

Given the diverse structure of boards and the demands of the many CEO's sitting on the boards of other companies, may not be held every month. Some boards meet every other month while other boards meet quarterly. And board meetings are not always good arenas for discussion. Enter committees. Between board meetings, committees of the board may handle issues and work. The board can assign committees authority to make board decisions while the board is away. But committees also serve as smaller, more manageable groups that can meet together more often in order to work through issues to be presented to the board. While the board's away, the committees will actually get things done.

All boards have an executive committee, which consists of officers of the company as well as outside directors. The executive committee is assigned the authority to act on behalf of the board between board meetings. This executive committee can be used for the approval of every-thing from an offering of securities that needs to go to market quickly to signatures on a land transfer.

Committees typically divide up the board's responsibilities. There is usually a finance com-mittee, responsible for review of financial per-formance. A human resources or compensation committee looks at everything from from the salaries of officers to issues like sick leave and vacation time. A nominating committee meets to consider candidates for the board. An environ-mental committee may be set up to supervise the company's environmental issues. The audit com-mittee will be responsible for verifying the com-pany's financial statements as well as control of internal audit functions.

These various board committees, usually con-taining three to five directors, can take the time to research and discuss an issue before it goes to the board for decision. For example, the finance com-mittee might take half a day to discuss the existing capital structure and develop a plan for reducing the debt of the company. The complexities of calling in existing bonds versus other methods of reducing debt is the kind of issue best examined in depth by the finance committee members and then presented briefly to the board with some simplified analysis and charts. Boards can rely on committees as forums for more open discussion.

Another benefit of committees of the board, apart from their convenience between meetings and creation of opportunities for more informal dia-logue, is that the committees can be used to achieve a certain degree of independence. Both the audit committee and the compensation com-mittee should have board members who are "independent directors" who are not officers and do not derive compensation from the corporation.

Defining an independent director, however, is not easy.

The Council of Institutional Investors offers this definition of an independent director:

- ◆ has not been employed by the corporation or an affiliate in an executive capacity within the last five years;

- ◆ is not (or is not a member of a company or firm that is) one of the corporation's paid advisers or consultants;

- ◆ is not employed by a significant customer or supplier;

- ◆ has no personal services contract with the corporation;

- ◆ is not employed by a foundation or university that receives significant grants or endowments from the corporation;

- ◆ is not a relative of the management of the corporation.

In their role as committee members, directors have the same fiduciary responsibilities as well as liability.

On the board's responsibility for preventing the books from being cooked

In 1993, when Leslie Fay, Inc. announced a reversal of its earnings for the previous three years, the chair of the company's audit committee explained that the financial accounting problems were news to him. He may indeed not have known of the accounting improprieties, but why not? Perhaps he should have known.

The supervision of those who prepare the books as well as the hiring and supervision of external auditors for the company are responsibilities that rest with the board. When accounting improprieties are discovered, shareholder questions understandably arise about the board and its supervision of the officers and auditors. When sales figures are inflated, the board holds ultimate responsibility.

At the same time, it is not reasonable to expect the board to uncover every irregularity before it occurs. Even the best supervision sometimes fails.

The keys to the adequate supervision of the financial reporting systems of a corporation are as follows:

- an audit committee comprised of independent board members

- regular meetings of the audit committee with discussions among members held without senior management present

- direct communication between the board audit committee and the company's external auditors

- board supervision of the scope and extent of the external audit

- audit committee review of the financial reports of the company before those reports are released to the public, including detailed looks at the rationale and reasoning in the segments of the financial reports that explain the numbers, called management's discussion and analysis

- head of the company's internal audit area reports directly to the CEO and has access to the board

- adequate supervision of the company's internal audit function including:
  1. Policies on what employees can audit, which areas and a rotation of those assignments
  2. Outside evaluation of the internal audit department of the company
  3. Adequate budget, resources and staffing for the internal audit department
  4. Logical scheduling of internal audits and priorities for completion of audits

When meeting independently with the company's outside auditors, the board audit committee should question them as follows:

- Did the external auditors have any disagreements with management on the financial reports?

- Did the external auditors find any material weaknesses in the company's internal control systems and were those weaknesses reported to senior management? What was the response? Are steps being taken to resolve the problem? Does senior management support the recommendations?

- Did senior management seek or obtain opinions from other external auditors on the financial statements? What issues were addressed by the additional auditors?

- Have the company's computer systems been reviewed to determine whether adequate controls are in place?

- How many former employees of the outside audit firm does the company employ and vice versa?

- What percentage of the outside auditor's business is the company's account? This factor can influence the independence of the auditor.

The board is an external force that can play a critical role in assuring the accuracy of the company's financial statements. Recently, Warren Buffett reflected dismay at the erosion of the transparency of financial statements in the United States. He bemoaned the fact that the United

States has always been known for its accurate reflection of corporate company performance but said that management creativity is booking earnings and postponing expenses had become so common that it constituted a "distortion du jour."

The result of such manipulation of financial results is the erosion of investor trust. Mr. Buffett joined with SEC Chairman Arthur Levitt in calling for the American Institute of Certified Public Accountants boards and senior management to self-regulate and provide financial statements that reflect accurately the financial status of the corporation. The board is a check point for halting the distortions du jour in the publicly-released financial statements of a firm.

There is one thing all boards have in common... they do not function.

Peter Drucker

KEY 20

Board meetings: art, science and requirements

Boards most commonly meet monthly, bi-monthly or quarterly. Most boards have an established date for meetings to allow directors to plan their schedules. Corporation law requires that notices be posted of board meetings, but board members may choose to waive notice in the interest of holding an emergency meeting between regular meetings. Generally the corporate secretary's office or office of legal counsel is responsible for the notice and scheduling of board meetings.

In most states board meetings can be held by telephone and all states require that a quorum, as established by the bylaws of the company, be present before the directors can begin conducting business.

The actual process of the meeting follows the rules of Parliamentary procedure and in situations in which there is disagreement and contention on the board, the rules of procedure can very often determine the results.

Board authorizations are required for everything from credit lines to securities offerings to the sale of land. Day-to-day business transactions such as contracts with suppliers can be delegated to the management team of the company but corporate-wide transactions require board authorizations. These authorizations come in the form of resolutions proposed, debated and then adopted by the board. Those resolutions can originate in committees. The resolution is the way the corporation, the artificial person, officially takes action. To authorize the use of this artificial person's funds, the board must follow formal procedures and issue official directions in the form of the resolution, which is the corporation's way of speaking to those who would do business with it.

All the procedural aspects of the board meeting are documented in minutes of the meeting kept by the corporate secretary. Board minutes should reflect motions, seconds to motions, discussions, abstentions and votes. The minutes should also reflect any entries and exits by directors and officers so that there is a permanent record of who was present during what discussions.

One thing board minutes need not reflect is the exact content of the discussions on issues. Board meetings are confidential for insider trading reasons as well as to ensure that discussions are candid and the board has the chance for free and open discussions.

Directors who vote against resolutions, abstain from voting due to conflicts or withdraw from meetings to avoid influencing board action should be certain that those actions are reflected in the minutes.

Shareholders versus stakeholders

The shareholder-stakeholder debate is one centered around ownership and authority. Who owns the corporation? Who has the authority to run the corporation? What rights do those who own the corporation have? What responsibilities do those who own the corporation have?

The traditional answer to all of the above questions is that shareholders own the corporation, had the authority to run it and can expect accountability and responsibilities as dictated by law. The fashionable answer to the question is that "stakeholders" have rights and authority in the operation of a corporation.

The term "stakeholder" had its origins in the 1930's when Professors Adolf Berle and Merrick Dodd staged their great shareholder vs. stakeholder debate. Mr. Berle believed that those who fork over the dough, risk-wise, should have the rights and responsibilities for running a corporation. In short, the shareholders own and run the corporation. Professor Dodd, who took a slightly different position, argued that there are "absentee owners" who represent society at large and should have some say in corporate operations. At a minimum, they had the right to hold the corporation accountable for its actions or inactions. The debate pretty much died the death of most academic debates: seven people read the research and by the end of the 1930's, the whole thing was pretty much forgotten.

In the 1960's, the Stanford Research Institute resurrected the issue by advising that, in a strategic sense, corporations should consider the interest of stakeholders, defined to be "those groups without whose support the organization would cease to exist." From this memo came modern-day stakeholder theory and its myriad of definitions as to who and what constitute stakeholders.

While the notion of shareholder is very clear, the notion of stakeholder remains a very fluid concept. The general definition is that a stakeholder is someone with a stake in the corporation: shareholders, of course, but also employees, customers, suppliers and communities in which corporations operate. Some theorists have even included competitors and the environment. For example, Professor Mark Starik has written an article: "Should Trees Have Managerial Standing?"

All of this fun obscures a fundamental distinction. The shareholder is a property owner who has invested funds with the expectation of a return. A stakeholder seeks to intervene in that property and contractual right simply because of an interest in environmental or community issues. There is no underlying contractual right for stakeholders and

Let me tell you something, this whole governance thing is getting pushed by institutional investors and academics, and between the two of them they couldn't run a *!#@&* hot dog stand.

Anonymous

their rights and interests create confusion rather than clarification.

The problems with stakeholder theory are as follows:

◆ No one is clear on the definition.

◆ No one has specified what the role of stakeholders should be vis-à-vis shareholders.

- How would stakeholders provide input to corporations and what would happen if there were disagreement among stakeholders themselves?

- How does the board weigh the input of stakcholders and what liability would they have for following the shareholders' vs. the stakeholders' desires?

- What would happen if stakeholders' desires resulted in losses to the shareholders?

- What will happen to the nature of the investment contract if stakeholders are allowed to intervene in corporate governance?

Nonetheless, the concept of stakeholders does bear on corporate decision-making. In a strategic sense, board members are well-advised to consider the impact of corporate actions on communities and employees before taking action. Companies are forced all the time to downsize because of new technology or competitive forces. Providing a plan for easing those downsized employees back into other jobs could benefit not just the employees but the company itself. By statute in many states, boards are permitted to consider the interest of stakeholders in determining whether to accept a takeover offer. The role of the company in a community can therefore be a valid factor in making a decision to reject a merger.

For corporate governance purposes, the theory of stakeholders remains an enigma. Directors should remain accountable to their shareholders and view stakeholder theory as a means for brainstorming during discussion sessions on critical strategic issues brought before the board.

KEY 22

The irate shareholder: annual ruckus

In the Vietnam War era, protestors often bought a share or two of Dow Chemical to use the 13as a forum to address Napalm, the war and general corporate decadence. While the causes have changed, shareholders still have their insurgent rights.

Under SEC regulations, shareholders have the right to submit proposals to be included in the proxy materials for vote at the annual meeting. These proposals are limited to 200 words and give the insurgents the right to speak at the annual meeting in support of their proposed action.

Types of shareholder proposals include requirements that directors own shares in the company, limitations on executive compensation and even procedural issues such as the timing of the annual meeting or release of the annual reports. The most common types of resolutions for 1999 annual meetings were:

- Executive compensation

- Staggered boards (proposals for both starting the practice and ending it)

- Cumulative voting proposals

- Independent director majority requirements

- Confidential proxy voting

(For an ongoing tally of the types of shareholder proposals, see www.socialfunds.com)

Other shareholder proposals are more concerned with social issues. For example, Cracker Barrel Cheese had a shareholder proposal to require the company not to discriminate against homosexual employees. Iroquois Brand Foods had a shareholder proposal that would have prevented the company from force-feeding geese and then rubber-banding their necks to increase the size of their livers to produce more paté.

Shareholder proposals have covered everything from doing business in South Africa to human rights in China. Electric utilities with nuclear plants face proposals to shut them down; consumer products companies are asked to stop testing their products on animals.

The shareholder proposal is often a focal point for political and social activism in which the company is only a convenient foil. While the SEC has the ability to exclude shareholder proposals as being beyond a corporate purpose, they have not taken an active role in vetoing proposals because even social causes can have an indirect impact on the company's bottom line. Board members should be prepared to discuss and address these issues prior to the annual meeting where the shareholders will have the chance to present their proposals and urge adoption.

Board reform:
rebels at the gate

Some of the large institutional investors in corporations are not at all satisfied that boards are
doing their jobs effectively. These institutional
investors have been led by CalPERS, the California
state employees' pension fund and one of the largest
stockholders in the country. Large investors are
beginning to use their clout to awaken boards and
directors to action, responsiveness and just generally paying attention to the business of the company.

Some institutional investors are advocates of the
stakeholder theory (see Key 21) and support the
involvement of community and employees.
Others advocate the two-tier German system in
which there is a board of directors for the company but also a shareholder advisory committee.
The Aufsichtrast is made up of institutional
investors of the company and it hires the
Vorstand, a management board. The shareholder
board is called Aktiengesellschaft.

One can only sympathize with Chrysler in its

merger with Daimler-Benz for it will surely take time just to determine who really is in charge. The theory behind the complex German system is to increase accountability and bring in directors with outside interests. In practice, it often results in stagnation as companies struggle to take action while facing so many different layers of governing agents.

While the debate on board structure continues, the concern remains the same: are directors and boards serving shareholders effectively? The answer perhaps does not lie in fundamental changes in corporate governance structure or the addition of new policies and procedures, but rather in the recruitment of effective board members. In a 1992 article entitled "Why Corporate Boards Don't Work," I listed the following qualifications to help to alleviate the concerns of shareholders and institutional investors about the capability and independence of corporate boards:

◆ Rely on outsiders who have no contractual, family or friendship connection with the corporation

◆ Look for qualifications: business experience; seasoned in everything from business setbacks to securities offerings to hiring and firing employees

◆ Look for someone with adequate time to commit to understanding the company and the industry and who will attend meetings

◆ Look for integrity and the ability to challenge the CEO and actions proposed to the board

Continuing monitoring of directors and their attendance is an important role for shareholders. The informed director who is present and accounted for can be a great catalyst for change. To be certain these qualities are present and accounted for and motivating action, some reformers have proposed the idea of an outside lead director. Other have proposed an annual self-evaluation by board members, which may include comments from managers as well as from the directors themselves on how well the board is performing.

Here are some other tools, with varying degrees of merit, suggested to improve corporate governance:

- ◆ Appoint some directors from outside the country to bring in international perspectives and encourage expansion overseas.

- ◆ Have separate individuals hold the positions of CEO and chairman of the board.

- ◆ Have the board evaluate the CEO annually.

- ◆ Make sure the board has a strong and independent executive succession plan

- ◆ Require directors to own stock.

- ◆ Insist that some compensation for directors be in the form of stock.

- ◆ Appoint a committee of independent board members to name candidates for board positions without relying on the CEO for nominations.

- ◆ Make sure that the board has planned for possible takeover by considering issues such as a staggered board, poison pills, shareholder rights' plan or super majority requirements and determined whether such defenses are in the best interests of the shareholders.

Good questions for good board members

R egardless of the company or industry, there are some questions in common that good board members should ask both to fulfill their fiduciary duties and ensure that the shareholders' investment in the company is protected:

- What was the average increase or decrease in executive compensation this year and how does that compare to the company's performance?

- What perquisites are given to board members and officers such as country club memberships, cars, apartments, autos and use of company airplanes?

- Does the company have hazardous waste or customers or suppliers with hazardous waste and how is the disposal handled?

- Has the company conducted an environmental audit to determine whether there are any unknown liabilities with respect to company property?

◆ Does the company have adequate insurance for environmental liabilities?

◆ Does the company have anti-discrimination protections in place? Are there adequate maternity leave policies that are in compliance with the law?

◆ Does the company have policies on sexual harassment and are they enforced?

◆ Is there adequate management of the company's pension and retirement funds?

◆ Are there any dangerous products the company sells and is there any litigation pending?

◆ Are there adequate internal controls in place? When was the last time an outsider reviewed those internal controls?

◆ Are there any pending government regulatory investigations? If so, what is the probable outcome of the investigation?

◆ Has the company changed any of its accounting practices and policies in the last year? If so, why?

◆ What portions of net income are due to unusual events?

◆ Were there any significant readjustments suggested as a result of the outside auditors' work?

◆ Does the company have adequate policies

and procedures in place with respect to insider trading?

◆ What litigation does the company face? What do the cases involve? Who is handling the case? What is the potential exposure if the case is lost?

◆ Does the company have a code of ethics and ethics training along with policies on conflicts of interest?

◆ Who manages the company's pension plan and what is their performance record?

There are a number of boards that have superb directors but lousy dialogue.

Henry Wendt

The best and worst in
corporate boards

A board asleep at the wheel is the worst corporate board. For example, the minutes of a Johns-Manville board meeting as long ago as 1932 reflected an awareness on the part of the board that there were serious health problems among asbestos workers. Such information did not bode well for a company whose one product was asbestos.

The workers were suffering from a disease called asbestosis caused by the inhalation of airborne asbestos particles. But the company and the board took no action for over 40 years when class action litigation had mounted to such a level that the company's outside auditors refused to certify the financial statements of the company without disclosure of the amount of liability exposure the company had. In the end, after years of living in denial about the nature of the company's product and the damage it can cause, Johns-Manville entered Chapter 11 bankruptcy. It eventually emerged from bankruptcy but has never recovered its sales and must still assign 25% of its profits to a trust fund to compensate workers for their disease and their families for their eventual losses. Litigation from building owners for the costs of the removal of asbestos still continues.

This was a case in which a board knew of an issue, understood its significance concerning potential liability, but chose to do nothing. Worse, it even pursued a course of conduct to conceal the information from shareholders, customers and workers. The qualities of integrity and independence from management were not present in the Johns-Manville board. The result was the near destruction of the company.

There are other companies in which boards perform in exemplary ways. For example, Scovill Corp., a brass company founded in 1803 when Thomas Jefferson was President, has evolved into a company with diverse product lines. It frequently calls employees and front-line salespeople into its boardroom for input and ideas. PPG encourages board members to challenge every aspect of management's conduct as well as its proposals for expansion or diversification. There is no hesitancy to speak on the part of PPG's board and the company's record of 100 consecutive years of dividends bears out the nature of its board and its effectiveness. The Stanley Works, yet another 100-year-dividend company, encourages ideas for innovation from everyone, including the board and has evolved over the years into a company with a reputation for consistent quality.

All good boards are the same: the directors challenge and confront because they devote the time necessary for preparation and participation and bring with them a rich body of business experience to assist management.

But unlike Tolstoy's unhappy families, all poorly-functioning boards are also the same. They are fraught with conflicts, have members who fail to attend meetings and are ill-prepared, have an atmosphere of cronyism and lack of independence. They are unwilling to challenge decisions and information. They fail to ask the questions necessary to get to the heart of corporate issues. The inevitable response of board members who find themselves dealing with a company with earnings reversals or litigation or malfunctioning products is: "I had no idea."

Indeed, that is the problem. That boards and board members make mistakes is not the issue. Of course they will and the rules concerning business judgment will protect them in those cases. But directors who fail to learn about fundamental corporate missteps are at the heart of poor corporate governance. Knowing what to ask and being willing to ask it is the role of every effective director. Their companies can only benefit from such vigilance.

INDEX

401(k) plans, 35

absentee owners, 75

abstention from a vote, 47, 48

accounting improprieties, 68–71

accounting practices and policies, 86

acquisition, lawsuits stemming from, 49–50

ADQ, 48

affirmatively reject opportunity rule, 45

Aktiengesellschaft, 81

American Institute of Certified Public Accountants, 71

annual meeting, 15, 26, 28, 37, 63, 78–80

annual reports, 11, 13, 15

anti-discrimination protections, 66

antitrust activities, 53

articles of incorporation, 11

audit committee, 66, 68, 69

Aufsichtrast, 81

bankers on boards, 20–21, 46–47

blackout periods for trading by directors, 60

blacks on corporate boards, 20

board authorizations, 73

board committees, 65–67

board meeting, 72–73

board member as shareholder representative, 46–47

board members, questions for, 85–87

board members, selection of, 20

board of directors, 11, 13–15

board reform, 81–84

board review of D & O coverage, 51

bonuses, 62

bookkeeping, adequate, 50

bribery, 53

Buffett, Warren, 23, 63, 70

business judgment rule, 41, 42, 49

business opportunities, capitalizing on, 44–45

by-laws, 31

candidates for board, 62

capital gains, 10

CEO, 20, 37, 61, 69, 82

CFO, 61

Chapter 11 bankruptcy, 52, 88

charitable contributions, 34

check kiting, 53

checks and balances, lack of adequate, 50

chief executive officer, 16, 61

chief financial officer, 16, 61

chief information officer, 61

chief operating officer, 61

CIO, 61

civil liability by directors, 56

civil penalties for insider trading, 60

class action lawsuits, 51

classes of directors, 30–32

Coca-Cola, 39, 51

code of ethics, 87

committees of the board, 65–67

company stock, as compensation, 62

compensation committee, 66

compensation consultants, 62

compensation for directors, 33–35

compensation of officers, 62–64

compliance officer, 61

computer systems, 70

conduct not covered by D&O insurance, 52–54
conduct of directors, 43
conduct, lawsuits stemming from, 49
conflict of interest, 35, 44, 46, 48
conflicts, 46–48
consulting fees, 35
consumer boycotts, 21
contracts, 12, 46–48, 73
COO, 61
cookies with raisins, accurate books, 52
cookies, fraudulent books, 52
cooking the books, 52, 68–71
corporate board, best and worst, 88–90
corporate board, make-up of, 19–25
corporate boards, independence of, 82
corporate directors as fiduciaries, 38–40
corporate funds, used for other activities, 52
corporate opportunity, who it belongs to, 45
corporate secretary, 61
corporate spending, controls on, 50
corporations, 9–11
Council of Institutional Investors, 67
Court of Committees, 16
credit lines, voting on, 47, 73
creditors, claims by, 10
criminal conduct by directors, 53, 56
criminal penalties for insider trading, 60
cronyism, 32, 90
D & O insurance, 49–51, 52–54
dangerous products, 86
deductibility of executive salaries, 63
deferred compensation plans, 35
director benefits, 31
director liability, 50
director's intent to take an opportunity, 45
directors, insider trading, 59–60
directors, removing, 36–37
disclose, 48
discloser of interest, 47
disclosure statement for directors, 57
discrimination lawsuits, 51
distortions in financial statements, 71
diversity in corporate boards, 21–23
dividends, 10, 28
dual role of directors, 44–45
East India Company, 16
election inspectors, 28
election of board, 13, 26–29
election of officers, 61-64
employment litigation, 50
employment practices liability, 51
environmental audits, 85
environmental committee, 66
environmental laws, violations of, 49
environmental liabilities, 53, 86
EPL, 51
Escott v. BarChris Industries, Inc., 56
ethics officer, 61
ethics training, 87
ethnic minorities on corporate boards, 20
executive committee, 65–66
executive compensation, 78, 85
executive search firms, 62
executor of an estate, 38
external auditors, hiring, 68
failure to diversify, lawsuits concerning, 49-50
failure to pay wage taxes, 54
fictitious person, corporations as, 12–13
fiduciary, duties of, 38–40
finance committee, 66
financial performance chart, 63
financial reports, 56, 69
financial statements, 47, 70
foreign representatives on corporate boards, 20

Form 10K's, 56
Form 10Q's, 56
Form 8K's, 56
former government officials on
    corporate boards, 20
Fortune 500, 20
Friedman, Milton, 63–64
gender discrimination suits, 51
general counsel, 61
General Motors, 16, 36
German system of board reform,
    81
government regulatory investiga-
    tions, 86
hazardous waste, 53, 85
human resources committee, 66
In re Caremark, 50
incentive plan, 62
incestuous business interconnec-
    tions, 47
incorporators, 11
independent director, 67, 79
influence on board decision, 48
informal removal of director, 37
information disclosure by
    director, 60
initial public offering, 55
insider trading, 56, 58–60, 73, 87
internal auditing, 69
internal controls, 86
    lack of adequate, 50
investment, 10
Investor Responsibility Research
    Center, 21
IRS, 55
issuance of securities, laws
    governing, 55–56
Kesner, Michael S., 64
lack of independence, 90
lawsuits and director liability,
    49–51
lawyers, 38, 46
levels of compensation, as share-
    holder issue, 63
Levitt, Arthur, 71
liability, 43
liability, corporate, 14
life insurance policies, 35
limitations on D&O coverage, 53

limited liability, 10, 11, 15, 41
litigation costs, 49
litigation pending, 86, 87
long-term profits, 57
maternity leave policies, 86
Mayflower Company, 10
MBCA, 14, 26, 37–38
meeting fees, 33
meeting procedures, 72
meetings, preparing for, 42–43
mergers, 43, 77
minutes of board meetings, 73
misleading information, release
    by directors, 60
mistakes, 41–43, 90
Model Business Corporation Act,
    14, 26, 37–38
multinational corporations, 16
negligence, 49
New York Stock Exchange, 23
nominating committee, 66
non-insider trading, rules about,
    59
notice of board meetings, 72
officers of the corporation, 11, 15
    numbered required, 61
outside auditors, evaluating, 70
ownership versus authority, 74
pay for performance, 64
payment in shares, 34
pension plans, 34, 86, 87
    missteps with, 53
performance, 15
performance shares, 34
performance-based stock options,
    34
Perot, H. Ross, 36
prerequisites for board members,
    85
personal liability by shareholders,
    14
personal liability for conduct, 52
Pilgrims, 10
political and social activism, 79
pooling agreement, 28
populist movement against
    undue privileges, 64
presentation of opportunity to
    board, 45

price fixing, 53

prison terms for insider trading, 60

professionals on corporate boards, 20

property ownership by corporations, 12

proprietary information, 38

protector, board as, 16, 18

proxy voting, 26, 79

punitive damages, coverage for, 51

question independence, 48

quorum of shareholders, 28

race discrimination suits, 51

racketeering, 53

readjustment, 86

rebel, the board as, 16, 17, 18

registration of securities, 55–56

replacing board members, 17

repositioning, 17

resignation of director, 37

resolution to remove director, 37

resolutions, adoption of, 73

responsibilities of ownership, 74

retainer fees, 33

retirement plans, 31, 34, 86

RICO violations, 53

rights of ownership, 74

risk, 10, 51

scheduling of internal audits, 69

SEC, 27, 55–57, 71, 78, 79

SEC v. Texas Gulf Sulphur, 60

secretary of the corporation, 28

Section 10(b) of SEC Act, 58, 59

Section 16 of the SEC Act, 57

Securities and Exchange Commission, 27, 55–57

Securities Exchange Act (1934), 27, 55–57, 58–60

securities filings, 13

securities fraud, 53

Securities Litigation Reform Act of 1998, 50

security offerings, 73

selecting directors, 23–25

self-regulation by board, 64, 71

settlement of lawsuits, 50

sexual harassment, 54, 86

shareholder activism, 32

shareholder dissent over compensation, 63

shareholder lawsuits, 53

shareholder proposals, 78–79

shareholder-stakeholder debate, 74-77

shareholders, 10, 11, 13, 15, 21, 26, 41, 82

shareholders as litigators, 50

shares,11

short-term profits, 57

slacker directors, 42

Smith, Adam, 9, 12

social issues, shareholder proposals concerning, 79

specialists on corporate boards, 20

staggered terms for boards, 79

staggered terms for directors, 31–32

stakeholders, 74, 76-77

stand-alone EPL policy, 51

Stanford Research Institute, 75

strategic initiatives, 13

strategist, board as, 16, 18

supervisor, board as, 16, 18

supplier as a board member, 46

tenure of board members, 30–32

time limits on board membership, 31

tippees, and insider trading, 59

traits, desirable in directors, 24

trustee of a trust, 38

unpaid obligations of the corporation, 14

utilities, 47

verdicts in lawsuits, 50

vice president for environmental, 61

vice president for human resources, 61

vice president for marketing, 61

Vorstand, 81

vote to remove director, 37

voting trust, 28

window periods for trading, 60

women on corporate boards, 19, 22–23

AUTHOR

MARIANNE M. JENNINGS, J.D., is a Professor of Legal and Ethical Studies in the College of Business MBA Program at Arizona State University. She is the author of five textbooks, including *Business: Its Legal, Ethical, and Global Environment* and *Case Studies and Reading in Business Ethics*. Her writing has appeared in *The Wall Street Journal*, the *Chicago Tribune*, and *Reader's Digest*, and her weekly column appears in newspapers around the country. She has served on four boards of directors and has been a commentator on National Public Radio's *All Things Considered*.